IMAGES
of America

UNION BEACH

IMAGES
of America

UNION BEACH

William H. Burket

ARCADIA

Published by Arcadia Publishing,
an imprint of Tempus Publishing, Inc.
2 Cumberland Street
Charleston, SC 29401

Printed in Great Britain.

Library of Congress Catalog Card Number: 98-87444

For all general information contact Arcadia Publishing at:
Telephone 843-853-2070
Fax 843-853-0044
E-Mail arcadia@charleston.net

For customer service and orders:
Toll-Free 1-888-313-BOOK

Visit us on the internet at http://www.arcadiaimages.com

CONTENTS

ACKNOWLEDGMENTS

This book is an outgrowth of a project of the Union Beach Memorial Library. Having had a lifelong interest in the history of Union Beach, it seemed to me that a calendar depicting scenes from the past might be one way to help preserve that history. In 1990, I brought that suggestion to the Library Association, the members liked the idea, and since 1991, the library has produced yearly historical calendars. Starting in 1993, the library has conducted two or three yearly "Walk Down Memory Lane" programs to collect oral history of the Borough and to collect and identify photos and other memorabilia, some of which are included in this book. Other photographs used are from the Borough's 50th Anniversary Committee material in the library collection; from the Heritage Committee of Florence Buchman and Ann Kofoed; and from the 1976 Bicentennial Committee, which I was privileged to chair. The year 2000 will mark the 75th anniversary of the Borough of Union Beach.

Thanks to Jackie LaPolla and the staff of the Keyport Library for their assistance in my research of the *Keyport Weekly* on film (1885–1972); Al Mirro for all the local photos he took over the years; Mrs. Ruth Walling for the loan of nine issues of the *Union Beach Record* newspaper, of which the Union Beach Library made copies; the Monmouth University Guggenheim Library for the photo of a local trolley*; the Perth Amboy Library and Monmouth County Park System; Bert Morris; Judy Gorhan Morris; Tom Gallo for information about trains; Tim Regan; Angel and Jack Jeandron; Joseph Collins III; Bob Belmonte of the Sand Bar Inn; Les Horner; Ann Kofoed; Mr. and Mrs. Frank Fuller; Bob and Gert Brunelli; Christine McKittrick Eastmond; Annabelle Guarino; Ruth Walling; Frank Mirro; Ronald Bezek; Mary Sauickie; Charles Van Chardrop; John Spielmann; Reverend Isabelle Wood; Dorothy Beaman; Clara Gilmartin; Alma Carnelli; Diane McNamara; Florence Van Rixoort; George Sappah; Bob Baird; Bill Perez; and everyone who heard about this book project and donated additional information or photos whom space does not permit listing individually.

Finally, I especially wish to thank Norma Kay for her invaluable assistance with the typing, editing, and layout of this book and the innumerable hours she spent at her computer and working with me on this project.

*For more information on the local trolley company, see *Jersey Central Traction Co.: Trolley to the Bayshore* by Joseph Eid.

INTRODUCTION

The area known as Union Beach has had a long and varied history beginning on May 22, 1676, when Richard Hartshorne purchased from the local Lenni Lenape tribe of Native Americans three necks of land which they called "Wacake," "Arowonoe," and "Conaskunck," the last of which is now the Borough of Union Beach. In August 1921, Native-American relics were found while grading some land on State Street (Florence Avenue) including a mortar and pestle, a tomahawk, and numerous arrowheads. Other items have been found at various times.

There was much activity in the area during the American Revolution with the British and Hessian soldiers stationed on Staten Island, the British in control of Sandy Hook, and the British fleet in the local bays. Colonel Tye and a party of almost 100 Loyalists landed at Conaskunck on June 20, 1780, capturing several patriots before the Monmouth Militia caught up with them as they were leaving.

George Poole and his son Richard, who was born in 1761, lived on the Poole family farm in what was then part of Middletown Township (now Union Beach). Both were members of the Monmouth County Militia, Richard joining as a drummer boy. In 1793, he was a lieutenant and in the War of 1812, he became Colonel Poole. He died in 1830 and is buried in the family plot in Holmdel. Poole Avenue is named after his family.

By April 4, 1924, an article in the *Keyport Weekly* discussed the tremendous growth of the New Jersey shore in the last 15 years from Laurence Harbor south, both in summer and year-round residences. Land in this area that had been farms was sold by developers for home sites. The property offered for sale in 1846 by the Florence & Keyport Co. was again offered for sale in 1915 as East Point Beach Estates and again in 1920 as Union Beach by Charles Carr. The Raritan Bay Realty Co. 1908 Union Subdivision (formerly the George Poole farm) was renamed Bay Shore Properties in 1911. Lots in the Lorillard Beach area, Flat Creek over to Union Avenue, were offered for sale in 1913. Those in Union Gardens, Poole Avenue over to Flat Creek, were offered for sale in 1917 and in Harris Gardens in 1920 by Nathan Harris. Charles Carr offered more lots for sale in 1920 in the area between Union Avenue and East Creek in Union Beach. It was not until the 1920s, with the new railroad station in 1923, that many people began to purchase lots and build homes. Many families relied on mass transportation to travel, as cars were just coming into their own. The last farm in town, the Slover farm, became Haven Park Homes in 1955, with Cottage Park Homes being built in 1956 on the last large piece of real estate in town. Since then, houses have been built on almost every empty lot with people either enlarging their homes or replacing them with modern buildings.

A bill introduced by Senator Stevens on February 23, 1925, to incorporate the Borough of Union Beach was signed by Governor George Silzer on March 16 that same year. The original petition included West Keansburg; however, Charles Carr and others opposed it and a modified bill was passed. After a special election, Union Beach gained its independence and the first Council meeting of the new borough was held on May 18, 1925.

During Prohibition, local rum runners had more powerful boats and knew local waters better than the Coast Guard. Boats would be unloaded on shore under the cover of darkness. Local residents reported it was not uncommon to hear gunshots in the night as the Coast Guard pursued the rum runners. The *Keyport Weekly* ran a story on January 31, 1930, about two boats off East Point. One boat sank with 500 cases of whiskey, while the crew of the second boat dumped 700 cases of whiskey overboard as they sped away. Local residents recovered large quantities, selling it for $10 to $35 a case. They also reported that the bottles were packed in straw and were labeled "Golden Dollar" and "Golden Girl." As fast as they could pull the cases ashore, they were taken away. There were stills in some of the houses in town as well as several speakeasies. Federal agents made a number of raids on local establishments.

The Union Beach municipal water system was installed in 1927. The Great Depression began in 1929 and as more and more residents were unable to pay their taxes, the new borough struggled during the 1930s to meet its financial obligations. At the request of the borough council, fiscal control of the borough and the school district were taken over on January 20, 1940, by the New Jersey Municipal Finance Commission (MFC). On March 6, 1975, the MFC declared the Borough of Union Beach financially solvent and removed its controls. A new water tower was completed in August 1980. The new borough hall/senior resource center was dedicated on January 4, 1981. The dedication of the new police headquarters adjoining the borough hall was held October 14, 1984. On March 27, 1992, the municipal water system was sold to the New Jersey American Water Company.

Being located next to the established town of Keyport, many local residents shopped and joined churches there. The early general stores in town did not survive and no lasting downtown area developed. The beach area was beautifully restored in 1996 and is now once more a very popular spot, crowded with sun worshippers during the summer months.

Some local phrases include the following: *around the Beach* means around town; *down the beachfront* refers to along Front Street; *on the other side of town* refers to the other side of Flat Creek, which divides Union Beach in half; and *live on the Beach* means to live in town.

I hope this book and the more than 200 photographs included reflect what life was like "on the Beach" from the early years of the community through the 1960s. I have lived in Union Beach all my life and have seen it go through many changes. Although it is vastly different now from when I was a boy, it is still a wonderful place to live and continues to have the community spirit which many towns seem to have lost.

One
THE EARLY YEARS

The Florence & Keyport Co. was incorporated on February 14, 1846. The company built a 2,200-foot-long pier at the foot of Dock Street in 1852, offered building lots for sale, and chartered the steamer *Armenia* to run trips to Union (now Union Beach) from New York in 1853.

This building at 338 Front Street is believed to be part of the Monmouth House Hotel erected by the Florence & Keyport Co. in 1852. Two other buildings that were originally part of the hotel are no longer standing. The house now has a deck on the second floor.

Of the five buildings in town that were researched and given plaques by the 50th Anniversary Committee in 1975, only three remain. One of these, the "Amos English House" at 1107 Florence Avenue, c. 1856, is now a private residence.

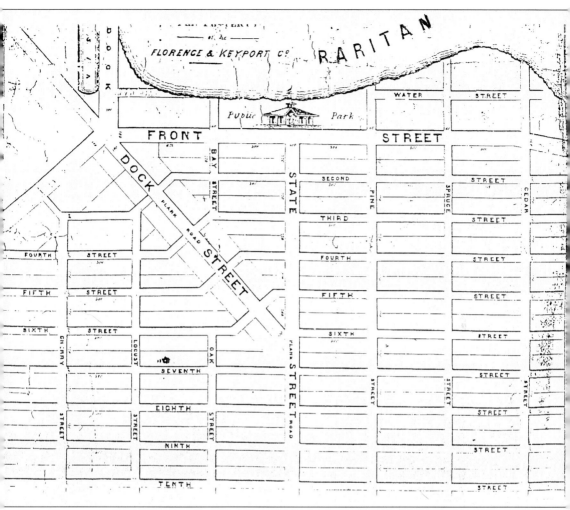

The Florence & Keyport Co. offered building lots for sale, laid down a wooden plank road (State Street), and built several homes on Dock Street. The stated purpose of the company was to build a road across the state of New Jersey to Florence, on the Delaware River. Only a few miles of the plank road were ever built to Keyport and the company soon ran out of funds. Originally, State Street (Florence Avenue) ended at Dock Street. It wasn't until many years later that Florence Avenue was extended to Front Street. Notice the shoreline in relation to Front Street. On this map, as well as on the East Point Beach Estates, Inc. map of this same area in 1915, there was no Center Street between Fourth and Fifth Streets.

Eleven-year-old Edna Booth is on the front porch of the Princess Cottage at 705 Front Street in 1914. Captain Arrowsmith of the *Eagle* may have built the house. The front porch has since been replaced by a stoop and the trees that provided shade that summer were removed long ago.

Some unidentified people, who may have been guests, sit on the bay side of the Princess Cottage. At one time, it was called the Lorraine Hotel. During the 1930s, the basement was used as a bathhouse and refreshments were sold.

Spencer Booth sitting on an iceberg by Princess Cottage in 1914. Two severe winter storms on February 20, 1914, and March 6, 1914, paralyzed the area. Raritan Bay was frozen over far across the bay, reportedly to Staten Island.

Three sisters—Marian, Edna, and Emma Booth—pose on top of the same iceberg. Train, trolley, and telephone service in the area were all interrupted during the storm.

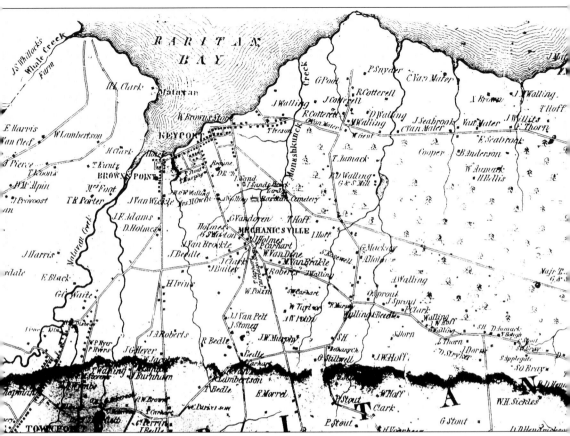

This 1851 Lightfoot map of Monmouth County shows the northern section of Raritan Township. Union Beach is the area north of Stone Road and east of the village of Keyport. Most of Stone Road became the new State Highway 36 in 1932. The only road showing in Union Beach is Poole Avenue. Chingarora Creek, labeled here as Monashkunck Creek, is the boundary between Keyport and Union Beach.

One of the five borough buildings given plaques by the Union Beach 50th Anniversary Committee in 1975, the Van Rixoort Booth house at 503 Dock Street was built in 1873.

This is a early postcard view of Poole Avenue, Union, Keyport, New Jersey, issued before 1925. Union Beach is still serviced by the Keyport Post Office with a Keyport zip code.

In 1908, the Raritan Bay Realty Co. offered lots for sale on the old 100-acre George Poole farm, which ran from Ninth Street south to the creek that crosses Florence Avenue, calling it the "Union Subdivision." In the April 28, 1911 edition of the *Keyport Weekly*, they offered two summer homes for sale. One was a small bungalow, 10 by 20 feet, and the second was a four-room cottage, 22 by 28 feet with a large attic and open porch for $1,500; $700 cash and the balance at $8 a month. Several of these cottages can be seen on Poole Avenue and Victoria Place. They have been added onto over the years.

In 1911, the area was renamed the Bayshore Properties and in 1913 a 4-by-6-inch booklet was produced featuring photographs of homes already built with letters from happy owners telling why they purchased property in Union Beach. Joseph Walling built a $5,000 house at 139 Poole Avenue. He felt the purchase was a good investment in a location convenient to train, trolley, steamboat, and the trading district. The area also featured easy access to fishing grounds.

Henry Walling Sr., father of Joseph Walling, built a home at 133 Poole Avenue because the area had low taxes, good water, and a "healthful location." The front porch has since been closed in.

The easy access to boating and fishing, a view of the bay, and low taxes were all incentives for Benjamin Bush when he built a house at 120 Poole Avenue. The front porch has since been closed in.

Joseph Schubert built a bungalow at 801 Seventh Street near Florence Avenue, c. 1922. His house may have been built on a site where a sand hill had been leveled and a number of Native-American relics were found in 1921.

The original wooden Union Avenue Bridge is shown here on an early postcard issued by Kumasaka's Department Store. The view is looking north on Matty's Creek (or Flat Creek). In 1930, the bridge was constructed that still stands today.

An early 1920s postcard shows cars parked by the beach along Front Street. The safe, gently sloping beach on Raritan Bay, located just a short commute away from jobs in the cities, was a major reason for people to locate their summer homes here. The railroad line was extended east from Keyport in 1890. The Jersey Central Traction Co. expanded trolley service east of Keyport in 1902.

The G.H. Jones Hardware & Lumber Store was at 614 Union Avenue, on the corner of Central Avenue. Mr. Jones served as the borough tax collector during the 1930s. The building had been vacant for a number of years when purchased in 1950 by Mr. and Mrs. Frank Mirro Jr. During the 1950s, the building housed the police department and the tax office. While Mr. Mirro was scoutmaster of Troop 56 during the 1950s, the troop's equipment was stored in the building's attic.

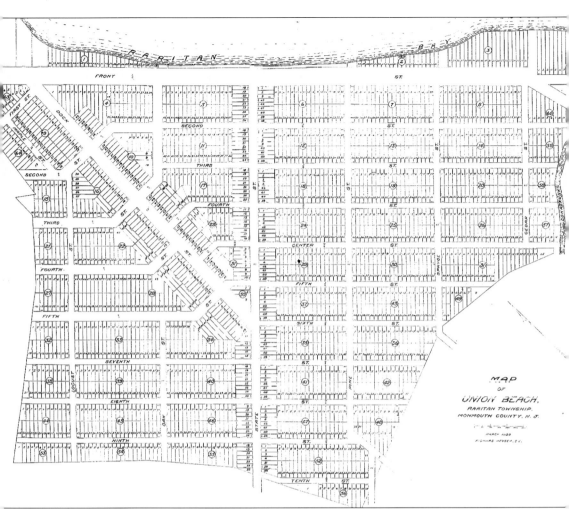

Developer Charles Carr sent out a 15-by-19-inch two-sided advertisement for Union Beach, in 1920. Carr was the man responsible for developing and selling much of the property in Union Beach, West Keansburg, and Keansburg. There is now a Center Street between Fourth and Fifth Streets. Notice also the coastline along Front Street as compared to the 1846 map. Flat Creek is labeled here as Conaskunk Creek.

The Fastest Growing Beachfront Development Along the Jersey Coast

UNION BEACH

3000 Lots

With over a mile of beautiful, white sandy bathing beach selling every day at the most remarkable bargain prices ever offered or that ever will be offered in the history of this seashore section.

THIS SEASON'S GREATEST OPPORTUNITY

The exceptionally beautiful bayfront location which Union Beach enjoys, its advantages of trolley, railway and main automobile highway right on the property; a natural boat harbor leading in from the bay at the foot of one of its main avenues, and from every one of its lots all of which are on or by the beach a clear uninterrupted view across the waters of Raritan Bay, one cannot help but exclaim: "Surely this is a great spot for the lover of bathing, boating and fishing!"

Union Beach offers not only the ideal seashore home site but a wonderful opportunity for investment.

MAIN OFFICE	OWNED and DEVELOPED	PROPERTY OFFICE
Laurel Avenue	by	Union Avenue
West Keansburg Beach	**CHARLES CARR**	Union Beach. N. J.
Keansburg, N. J.		

WATCH UNION BEACH GROW

Charles Carr was also using the name Union Beach to sell land east of Union Avenue over to East Creek where the 104-acre John Carr farm had been. The 1885 farmhouse remains at 712 Beachview Avenue. The section of town between Flat Creek and Union Avenue was called Lorillard Beach and lots were offered for sale in 1913.

A modern photograph shows the one-story building that was James Cleary's store at 1131 Florence Avenue. From 1937 to 1952, it was the home of the Community Shoe Repair Shop of Nicola Buccino and for many years now it has been a residence. The two-story building next to it, built in the early 1930s, was George and Marion Divens' general store, and later the home of Carmen's Deli & Catering.

JAMES CLEARY'S STORE

Florence Avenue
UNION   Keyport

Fink's Pork Sausage, lb · ·	30c
Pork Chops, lb. · · ·	28c
Cala Hams, lb. · · ·	14c
Bacon, lb. · · · ·	25c
No. 7 Copper Bottom Wash Boiler	1.00
No. 7 Brooms · · ·	60c
Ladies Tamoshantas · ·	50c
Men's Winter Caps · ·	1.00
Men's Winter Gloves · ·	20c
Blue Eye Matches, box · ·	5c
Babbitt's Soap, cake · ·	5c
Toys and Dolls at Bargain Prices.	
Other Things · too numerous to mention.	

This advertisement for James Cleary's store is from the November 9, 1923 issue of *Keyport Weekly*. Many local residents had their mail delivered to the store for convenience.

22

An old postcard shows summer bungalows built on Ninth Street looking toward State Street (Florence Avenue). In the photograph are, from left to right, 817, 819, 821 and 827 Ninth Street. Over the years, the owners have built additions and winterized the houses.

The store at the corner of Union and Columbia Avenues has been the home of several businesses over the years. In the 1920s it was the Fitzsimmons Hardware Store, and William Rosine sold vegetables here in the 1930s. Phil's Market, owned by Phil Bommer, sold meats and groceries in the 1940s and 1950s. When Phil retired, it became Jim's Food Market and then Pluggy's Place. The two storefronts on the right of the photograph are now an empty lot. In June of 1946, Heintz & Kology, Inc. opened a store selling General Electric appliances and records. In the 1950s, the building housed the Holy Family Parish Hall while the new church was being constructed. In the background is the old 1927 water tower. (The Dorn Collection.)

This sign on Stone Road (Route 36) advertised lots for sale in Harris Gardens in 1920. The view is looking north toward the railroad tracks.

The construction of the first house in the Harris Gardens section of town at Patterson Avenue and Stone Road (Route 36) was photographed here in April 1920.

The F.K. Hill home in Harris Gardens was completed and occupied in April 1920. In back of the house is a concrete block shop. Harris Gardens is east of East Creek over to Natco, Rose Lane, and south of the old railroad tracks.

Mrs. Catherine Rehbein of Harris Gardens helps her daughter get a drink at the water pump. Union Beach was well known for its excellent drinking water.

Mrs. Catherine Rehbein is here with her son Harry and their chickens in the 1920s. Many local residents kept chickens in the 1920s to the 1940s. You could still hear a rooster or two crowing in the early mornings in the late 1950s.

Harry Rehbein is providing water for his ducks. Some residents kept ducks, some had geese, and there were a number of families who kept cows during the 1920s. One resident, John Sauickie, raised pigs, butchering them each fall.

This Kumasaka Department Store postcard of the 1920s looks east along Front Street at the intersection with Dock Street. The number of parked cars indicates it was another busy day at the beach.

The first Union Beach branch of the Keyport Post Office opened on November 1, 1921, to serve Union Gardens, Union Beach, Lorillard Beach, and Harris Gardens. It was located inside the store owned by Charles D. Parry at 711 Union Avenue. Residents in the Union section either had mailboxes along Florence Avenue for rural delivery or they had their mail delivered to Cleary's store for pick-up.

The Lorillard & Union Beach Improvement Association was organized on July 30, 1920. They purchased a building at Cambridge and Union Avenues to house a fire company and to provide a hall for use by the growing community. The Union Beach Fire Co. No. 1 was organized on November 15, 1922. In 1929, the building became the borough hall. From left to right are Ernest Bade, Harry McCandless, Emil Friewald, and Fred Clauss.

In 1921, local residents wait for the train near Mondorf's store on Union Avenue before the railroad station was built. The 1925 train schedule listed stops at both Natco and at the new Union Beach station. The 1898 and 1905 schedules listed only a stop at Lorillard (the Lorillard Brick Works), which is now Rose Lane.

"The Lorillard and Union Beach Improvement Association appointed a committee to go before the Raritan Township Council for a bridge to span Flat Creek to the Railroad Station." (From the minutes of the association, May 25, 1923.) It is unfortunate that only a part of the minutes of this organization survive and that the secretaries from 1920 until 1929 recorded only a portion of what must have transpired. From an early postcard, we know that the bridge was built at Central Avenue.

A group of people swim near their sailboat at low tide off of Conaskonk Point. You could rent a tent or a tent site for a short vacation.

This photograph of Joseph and Mary McNamara was taken in 1926 at 511 Shore Road, which was the summer home of their grandparents, Thomas and Annie McNamara of Elizabeth, New Jersey. The tent in the background served as the summer home of their son Thomas.

The Union Beach Record
YOUR HOME PAPER—PUBLISHED IN THE INTEREST OF UNION BEACH

VOLUME 10—NUMBER 11   UNION BEACH, N. J., JULY 13, 1934   PRICE 4 CENTS

NO TYPHOID IN BAY WATERS

Union Beach Fireman Given Final Warning By State Assn.

Says Mortuary Benefit Will Be Lost Unless Physical Examinations Are Taken

In our issue of June 22nd we reprinted a letter from the secretary of the state Firemen's Relief Association in which it was made clear to all firemen that a law was passed at the 1923 convention requiring all new members to undergo a physical examination and get a certificate from the examining doctor on the form issued by him. On and after December 1, 1930 these examination reports must be made out on a specific form supplied by the State Association which will be supplied to the secretaries of all volunteer fire companies upon request.

It is up to the company secretaries to see that they get these forms to supply to members upon

EDWARD W. CURRIE GETS STATE APPOINTMENT

Matawan's Chief Executive Made Assistant Attorney General By Wilentz

Attorney General David T. Wilentz, of Perth Amboy has named Mayor Edward W. Currie of Matawan as an assistant attorney general. Announcement of the appointment of Matawan's mayor was made Wednesday by Mr. Wilentz's office in Trenton. Mayor Currie has been assigned to the department of agriculture.

Mayor Currie is a native of Keyport. He is a graduate of Princeton University and entered the

Says Scare Was Started by Radio Announcements by N. Y. Ban in Polluted Waters

As a result of the action of New York state in prohibiting bathing in the Staten Island Sound on the grounds that the waters are polluted considerable concern has felt in this borough and immediate vicinity over the safety of swimming in Raritan bay.

However it seems to be much ado about nothing for Dr. Charles S. Thompson Perth Amboy health officer said that no cases of typhoid had been reported as a result of bathing in local waters.

Dr. Thompson declared only one case of typhoid fever had been reported and that was early in May—long before the swimming season opened. Records in the health department reveal that not since early in 1920 had there been an outbreak of typhoid. There were about nine cases at the time and none of them was the result of bathing. They were more or less traced to a "carrier."

As far as can be ascertained no

Matawan Police Officer Is Fooled By "Paralytic" Faker

LACK OF COLLECTIONS IS KEYPORT'S DIFFICULTY

Delinquent Taxes and Water Bills May Force Borough to Default

Keyport will have a deficit of $10,000 on August 1 if the delinquent taxes and water bills are not paid by that time, according to a report made by Councilman Albert M. Haigh, chairman of the finance committee, at the meeting of the mayor and council held Monday night.

The borough will owe $7,923.75 in bonds and interest on that date and unless money is collected Councilman Haigh stated the borough would probably default on its debts.

Councilman Justus R. Camp reported that the reading for the

Ill Man Who Invades Matawan Headquarters Proves to Be Fake

Officer Ritter Johnson of the Matawan police department has always had faith in human nature, but after his experience on Tuesday night, he says he will have to be shown hereafter before he extends his sympathy to anyone. It was not until yesterday that Officer Johnson would discuss how he had been taken in by a "faker" even to the extent of call ing a Catholic priest to the jail to assist him as well as a physician.

Johnson says it was about 9 o'clock Tuesday night when a young man apparently a victim of paralysis, was led up to the door of the borough hall by a respectable citizen who had found him moving slowly along the street.

The *Union Beach Record* was published weekly from 1925 to 1947 by Albert Cowling Sr. at 351 Bayview Avenue. In 1936, the cost was 4¢; in 1947, it was only 3¢. The borough council encouraged Mr. Cowling to start the paper in 1925 to help unify the new borough. The library is now looking for surviving copies of the newspaper.

Two

THE COMMUNITY DEVELOPS

In May 1925, Mayor Charles Miller and the four-man police force led the first Memorial Day parade up Union Avenue. They had only one more block to go to the borough hall/firehouse at Cambridge Avenue. It wasn't until 1928 that Union Avenue, Front Street, Florence Avenue, and Broadway were paved and became county roads.

This photograph was taken outside the Lorillard and Union Beach Improvement Association Hall/Union Beach Fire Co. No. 1 firehouse on Election Day for the first mayor and council on May 12, 1925. Where are the ladies who regained the right to vote in New Jersey in 1920?

The first mayor and council of the borough of Union Beach in 1925 were, from left to right, Russell Wells (school principal), Frederick V. Schober, James P. McKittrick, Mayor Charles Miller, Frederick Clauss, John Staley, and Burtis Aumack.

The newly elected officials in the first regular election of the new borough of Union Beach in November of 1925 were, from left to right, Councilmen Fred Schober, John A. Spielmann, Cyril Farley, Mayor James P. McKittrick, Fred Clauss, Thomas Lynch, and Burtis Aumack. The photograph was taken outside the Union Hotel at Union and Sydney Avenues. Boy Scout Troop 56 was chartered in March 12, 1925.

The members of the Union Beach Fire Co. pose with their first fire truck on May 26, 1923, outside of the firehouse/hall. The first Roman Catholic Mass in Union Beach was said on August 22, 1922. During the week of September 8, 1933, Chicago Presbyterian Evangelist Rev. Oscar Lowry Sr. packed the hall for revival meetings sponsored by the local churches. His son, a senior in divinity school, was also serving as the minister of the First Congregational Church.

33

In 1929, the Catholic Club purchased the 1830 farmhouse owned by Mr. and Mrs. Willis Aumack, using a third party. The Bishop chose the site, on Route 36, for the location of the new Roman Catholic church. The clubhouse was used for meetings and fund-raising activities with caretakers, Mr. and Mrs. William Cole, living on the top floor. After the church was built, the old house was removed in the mid-1940s to provide parking spaces.

The ground was broken in 1941 for the first Holy Family Roman Catholic Church of Union Beach. A year later the church, designed as a small Mission church, was completed. It had a seating capacity of 200. In June 1942, Rev. Walter Slattery became its first pastor. The church became a parish on June 11, 1942.

On Sunday, June 26, 1955, the present Holy Family Church was dedicated. It was built around the original church at a cost of $200,000 and seats approximately 600. In 1960, beautiful Bacilican bells replaced the original chimes. On November 28, 1965, ground was broken for the Holy Family Parochial School on the Hazlet side of Route 36.

The Grace Methodist Episcopal Church building was dedicated on February 13, 1927. Reverend John C. Parsons was the pastor. The church was remodeled and an educational wing was added in 1959. Sunday school had been held in the old one-room schoolhouse by the Keyport Calvary Methodist Episcopal Church from 1860 to 1870 and again from 1895 to 1915. After Sunday school, the two teachers would walk back to Keyport to attend morning worship.

The First Congregational Church, was located at 623 Central Avenue, and held its first service in its new church on October 30, 1927. The first Sunday school session was held on November 14, 1926, and the first service took place on December 12, 1926, at the firehouse. When the church merged with the Methodist church on Pentecostal Sunday, June 5, 1960, the sale of this building paid off the debt of the Methodist church. The building is now a private residence.

The Grace Methodist Church and the First Congregational Church were merged on June 5, 1960. Both churches could trace their beginnings back to the cottage prayer meetings, which began on October 26, 1922, at the Florence Avenue School with visiting ministers from local churches. Before that, a tent had been used for services at Seventh Street and Florence Avenue.

The Full Gospel Mission Church was founded about 1930 on Front Street. The name was later changed to the Union Beach Pentecostal Church. In 1947, it relocated to this building at Union and Sydney Avenues, which had been Walling's Delicatessen in the 1920s.

A new church building was constructed in 1981 next to the old building on Union Avenue and the name was changed to the Faith Chapel, Interdenominational. In 1995, an all-purpose room and an apartment for Rev. Isabelle Wood were added on the right side of the church.

The Daisy Girl Scouts pose for a picture before the start of a parade in the early 1930s. Juanita Nyack is the flag bearer. The banner holders, from left to right, are Catherine Simmons, Carolyn Wiersing, Kate Miller (the leader, without a hat), and Dorothy Miller. In the background is Paul Kolodziej's Florence Restaurant at the corner of Florence and Broadway, across from the old trolley barn.

Phone Keyport 1139   Paul Kolodziej, Prop.

FLORENCE RESTAURANT

BAR AND GRILL—PICNIC GROVE

GOOD BEER, WINE AND LIQUOR

Two Minutes From Bathing Beach

Use of Grove Free to Clubs or Organizations

Florence Ave. (At Broadway)   Union Beach, N. J.

This advertisement for the Florence Restaurant appeared in the July 13, 1934 *Union Beach Record.*

Schober's Seafood Restaurant was on the corner of Union Avenue and Stone Road (Route 36) from the 1920s to the 1940s.

Schober's became Sarah Bee's Restaurant and the Brunelli & Smith Service Station in the 1940s. On March 23, 1950, McCluskey's Restaurant was badly damaged when the gas station, then operated by Walter Metzger, was destroyed by fire. The building then became a Mary Carter's Paint store until it was demolished to provide more parking space for the People's National Bank branch office.

The Associated Veterans of American Wars, Post No. 1, Union Beach, was chartered on December 6, 1925. The Ladies Auxiliary was also organized. On Memorial Day, 1929, their post home on Jersey Avenue was dedicated. American Legion Post 321 sold the hall in 1959 and the building was destroyed by a fire a few years later. The hall's flagpole now stands at the Memorial Library building. From left to right in the first row, on the hall's front steps, are Gus Dirner, Harry McCandless, Frank Mirro, and Bill Tighe.

Members of the Women's Regular Democratic Organization are shown here c. 1933. From left to right are as follows: (front row) unidentified, Sadie Mount, Mrs. John Cooney, Mrs. Betz, Mrs. Gryner Scholer, and Mrs. James Farrell; (second row) unidentified, Elizabeth Spielmann, Secretary, and three unidentified women; (third row) Jennie Miller Spielmann, unidentified, Mrs. Samson, Mrs. Verna Schober Opanowicz, two unidentified women, Beatrice Pouzenc, President, Mrs. ? Cherney, and Mrs. Helen Taka; (back row) six unidentified ladies.

A cow belonging to Mrs. Susie Youncosky and Marion McKittrick (who became the author's mother) check each other out sometime in the 1920s. The several cows kept in the community provided fresh milk for some of the local families. There was no 2% milk in those days.

"The Union Beach Women's Regular Democratic Club made a trip Tuesday morning in a large bus for Freehold where they were the guests of Sheriff Howard Height. After a visit to the jail, they were served a luncheon." (*Keyport Weekly*, April 7, 1933.)

CLEAN-UP WEEK
FOR UNION BEACH
AUGUST 29 TO SEPTEMBER 3

PLEASE SHOW REAL PUBLIC SPIRIT AND
CLEAN UP YOUR PREMISES

COLLECTION SCHEDULE—Rubbish, (not garbage) will be collected according to the following schedule. If you miss the collector the first day he is in your section be sure to be ready the second day. TWO DAYS ONLY will be spent in each section.

MONDAY and TUESDAY, August 29, 30—Stone Road to Beach front, West of Conaskunk Creek to Keyport Line, which includes Union Park, Bayshore, Union, Cottage Park, Union Gardens and West Union Beach Sections.

WEDNESDAY and THURSDAY, August 31, Sept. 1—Stone Road to Conaskunk Creek on West Side of Union Avenue, which includes the Lorillard section.

FRIDAY and SATURDAY, September 2, 3—Stone Road to Bay, North of Union Avenue, including Union Beach (east), Harris Gardens and Natco sections.

Rubbish must be placed in receptacles on curb in front of your premises. (Barrels, boxes or any other receptacle will be emptied by the driver and returned to the owner.) We would like to urge that the summer visitors take advantage of cleaning their premises before returning to their city homes. In this manner they will help the year-around folks to protect their property while they are away from the Borough.

For further information telephone any of the following persons: Joseph Smith, 724-J; Alfred Mirro, 542; Russell V. Wells, 743-M; or see any member of the Board of Health or Inspectors.

CHARLES SAMPSON, Inspector

The year is unknown for this "Clean-up Week" notice. Flat Creek is listed as Conaskunk Creek. In 1932, most of Stone Road became Route 36.

Bluebird Park was located at Jersey and Union Avenues during the 1920s. It contained a merry-go-round, wheels of chance, Skee Ball, refreshments, a tavern ("The Blue Bird"), and the Black Cat Dance Hall. There was fun for everyone. The amusements were later moved to the beachfront.

In 1936, the Union Beach Congregational Church Summer Bible School was held in the Cottage Park School on Morningside Avenue. Mrs. Mildred Yost was one of the teachers under the supervision of the Rev. Pierce. Rev. Pierce later became a missionary to Africa.

In the 1920s and 1930s, the only way to open Union Avenue without a snowplow was by residents working together. Snow is shown here being cleared from in front of the borough hall/Union Beach Fire Co. No. 1 home at Cambridge and Union Avenues, *c.* 1930.

The second site of the Union Beach Branch of the Keyport Post Office in 1925–1926 was at Charles Sappah's store at Central Avenue and Spruce Street, just down the street from the railroad station.

An early Miss Union Beach, Jeanette Roche, poses along with her four escorts, the two Weber brothers on either end and John Mount and Ray Menges in the center

Mr. Alfred Mirro's barbershop and spaghetti restaurant on Union Avenue is shown here in a photograph taken after 1925. In the 1950s, before he retired, the barbershop was on the other side of the building than that shown here.

This is an interior view of the barber shop. When Mr. Mirro retired, he was still charging boys 50¢ for a hair cut.

A footbridge crosses the creek at the end of Bay Avenue. For years, the residents of Bay Avenue had maintained a walkway and bridge to Pebble Beach.

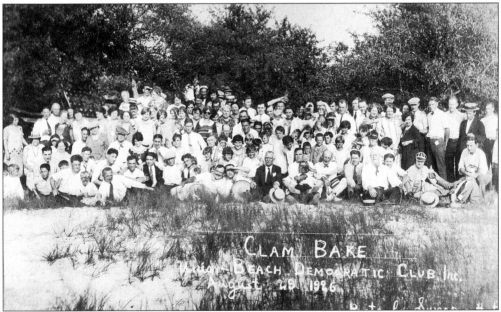

The Union Beach Democratic Club was organized on June 3, 1925, with 70 charter members. In the November 1925 election, only one Republican, Fred Schober, was elected. The club held a clambake on August 28, 1926. Mayor McKittrick, in the front, is leaning on his right elbow while Councilman Fred Clauss is leaning on his left elbow.

The photograph on this old postcard was taken looking north on Union Avenue at Central Avenue. On the corner is Kumasaka's Department Store and next door is the A&P Grocery Store.

This postcard view of Mrs. Leahem's, Crescent Grove, shows bungalows, which could be rented by summer visitors.

Beach View Avenue is shown here in a postcard view with little John Spielmann looking back at his uncle, Charles Spielmann, while other members of the family look on.

Sadie Mount's ice cream and candy store was located on Union Avenue. It later became the home of John Mount and is now the site of the Faith Chapel.

This is a close-up view of a tent on a wooden platform used by a family on Central Avenue. At the end of summer, the tent was packed away until the following year.

The home of Mr. and Mrs. James P. McKittrick on Central Avenue has the summer tent up on a wooden platform. Besides being cooler than the house on hot summer nights, the tent also provided extra space for visiting relatives from the city.

Playing on the see-saw in front of the brick house built by Joseph William McNamara at 808 Park Avenue are his children, Joseph and Mary McNamara, and their aunt, Isabelle Peterson of Elizabeth. The image was taken c. 1929.

It looks like the McKittrick family is going to have chicken for supper. They may also have had some of the wild growing asparagus from their yard, a crop that Mr. John Carr had grown on his farm before it was divided up into building lots.

Part One

1. Opening by ....Miss L. Daniels
Stage-Door Johnnie .... Isabelle McLellan

Stage Steppers

Burtina Aumack   Eleanor Sappah   Evelyn Scholl
Octavia Aumack   Ethel Clarihew   Carolyn Wiersing
Isabelle Hedley   Annaclaire Masson   Betty Ward
Virginia Liekefet   Dorothy Wills   Florence Dennebaum
Christina Barclay

2. A Baby Doll	Eleanor Cullen
3. Jazzland	Annaclaire Masson
4. Our Singers	Aumack Sisters
5. A Bit of Sunshine	Ruth Walling
6. Dance	Evelyn Scholl

7.   **Toe Dancing Land**

(a) Soldiers	Aumack Sisters
(b) A Petite Miss	Isabelle Hedley
(c) Heart Stealers	Evelyn Scholl

Isabelle McLellan   Ethel Clarihew
(d) A Heart's Desire ....   Ruth Walling
8. Our Own Pat Rooney .... Dorothy Wills
9. Valse Acrobatique ... . Octavia Aumack

10.   **Farmer Land**

Christina Barclay   Eleanor Sappah   Annaclaire Masson
Isabelle Hedley   Ethel Clarihew   Burtina Aumack
Evelyn Scholl

11. Rachel and Ruben   Florence Dennebaum
Dorothy Wills
12. She's A Great Great Girl .... William Daniels

This is part of the program for the second recital given by the pupils of Miss Lillian Daniels' Dancing School on Friday evening, July 6, 1928, at Union Firehouse. Miss Daniels ran a dance studio in Newark, but in the summers she had a studio at Central and Ocean Avenues. Lessons were given on Tuesdays and Wednesdays for 50¢. Miss Daniels had some 47 pupils.

The 1933 Union Beach Kubs included the following players from left to right: (in front) Stanley Przygocki (batboy); (second row) Jim McKeon, Wilber Klaiber, Mike Yankoski, Francis "Skeets" Corcoran, Will Hayes, Victor Yankoski, and John Yankoski; (back row) Leonard Carpentier (coach), Phillip Scholl, Edward Bausback, Anton Yankoski, Michael Strano, George Pouzenc, Mike Levine, Jim Sullivan, Clifford "Chink" Klein (pitcher), and Tom Corcoran (score keeper).

The 1934 Anchor Inn baseball team included the following from left to right: (front row) Charles Thomas, John Cherney, John Calandriello, Joe Gross, George Heitzenrolder, George Cowling, and George Pouzenc; (back row) Bill Gardner, Bill Hedley, Vic Murauskos, Teddy Trembley, Michael Sullivan, Donald Abrams, and Gus Dirner Jr.

This is a side-view of the steam shovel used to dig clay out for the manufacture of bricks and clay tiles by the National Fireproofing Co. (Natco) in the Natco section of Union Beach. Local resident Walter Austin was one of the men who operated this equipment. Some of the rails and old equipment remain under the water of Natco Lake.

A Lorillard brick made by the Lorillard Brick Works (1887–1901) sits on top of four different clay tiles that were probably produced in Natco by the National Fireproofing Co. (1901–1929). Local residents used these tiles for the foundations of their homes, as well as for the wall and floor construction of garages.

The smooth Natco tile used in the construction of Letwenske's garage at the corner of Florence and Bay Avenues reportedly wasn't made at the Union Beach Natco plant but at their Perth Amboy plant. Letwenske's trucking company transported the finished tiles.

This scenic view shows 90-acre Natco Lake, two-thirds of which is located north of Route 36 in Union Beach. High-quality clay was mined here for the production of Lorillard bricks and Natco tiles. Digging on the Hazlet side began in April of 1919. Operations ceased in 1929. Today the old clay pits, filled with water, serve as a wildlife refuge.

The houses that used to line Natco Lane (now Rose Lane) were built by the Lorillard Brick Works to house their employees. This house, the larger of the two that remain standing, was built for the foreman. Over the years, IFF has been purchasing these houses and demolishing them one by one. The house that had been on the corner of Rose Lane and Jersey Avenue also served as the company store for employees.

The surviving duplex house on Rose Lane was originally built for brick workers. Some of the houses were occupied by a single family, others were occupied by two families. In 1949, 21 families were living on Rose Lane; today, only 4 live there.

Lavoie Industries of Morganville purchased the Natco site on December 9, 1948, for $15 million. In October 1950, the site was sold to Van Ameringen-Haebler, Inc. of Elizabeth and work began to prepare the site for a new factory. In December of 1958, the company merged with Polak & Schwarz and became International Flavors & Fragrances.

This photograph of the IFF Research & Development Center on Route 36 shows the original section of the building under construction in 1967. The building has been enlarged twice over the years. Later IFF would construct two additional buildings on the Hazlet side of Route 36.

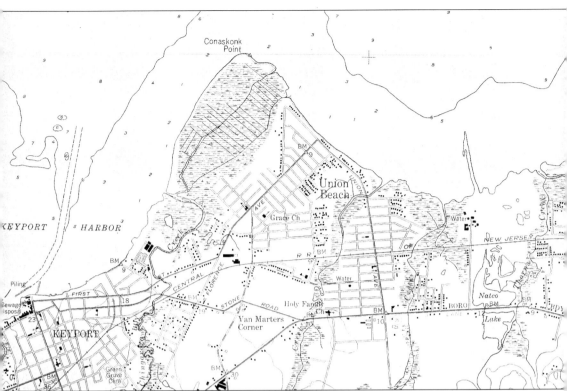

This topographic map of the Union Beach area was prepared in 1954 by the U.S. Geological Survey. JCP&L purchased 134 acres of Conaskonk Point in December 1967 for the construction of a nuclear power generating station. The plans were shelved in May of 1968. On June 29, 1972, JCP&L obtained a permit to construct two 400,000-kilowatt generating stations. Nothing has ever been built on the Point. Natco Lake is the former site of the old clay pits of the Lorillard Brick Works and later the National Fireproofing Co. The clay pit south of Route 36 in Hazlet wasn't dug until 1919. All that remains of the 1887 Lorillard Brick Works 4,000-foot pier is a sand bar and pilings sticking out of the water in the bay. With the formal opening of the Garden State Parkway on October 24, 1954, the area was transformed from farmland to rows and rows of new houses, highway strip malls, jammed local highways, and schools on half-sessions.

This certificate showing Dora Carr's ownership of 64 shares of the Keansburg-Union Beach Realty Co., dated May 5, 1930, was signed by company president Charles Carr and company treasurer Ernest Bade. The shares were sold on August 13, 1945, to local real estate agent John M. Friel. Charles Carr developed much of the property in the Union Beach, West Keansburg, and Keansburg areas.

The IFF fragrance chemical manufacturing plant was built on the site of the old brick works at the foot of Rose Lane. In 1997, most of these operations were moved to Georgia. The Union Beach plant is being converted into a bulk packaging and shipping facility. (The Dorn Collection.)

Three
TRAINS AND TROLLEYS

"The Central Railroad is building a railroad station in Union Beach to replace a small temporary station in use for a few months." (*Keyport Weekly*, August 4, 1922.) One ticket agent was on duty most of the year, but during the summer months two agents were on duty. Most families still relied on mass transportation to get around. The station was located on the north side of the tracks. Spruce Street was a dead end street at the station. Jake Cunuek was the agent in 1924.

Mrs. McKenna, the grandmother of Annabelle Cherney Guarino, was hired to run the newsstands at both the Union Beach and Keansburg railroad stations from 1924 to 1929. Items sold included newspapers, magazines, candy, cigarettes, etc. The station was heated in the winter by a pot-bellied stove. A fire Saturday night, April 26, 1958, destroyed the railroad station. It was replaced by a shed for passengers.

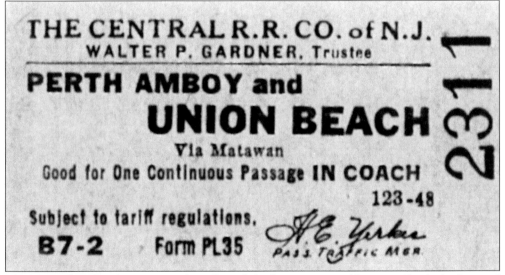

This Central Railroad one-way ticket allowed the bearer to travel between Perth Amboy and Union Beach. Before the arrival of highway strip malls in the 1950s, local people did most of their shopping in Keyport, Red Bank, or Perth Amboy.

INFORMATION

This Railroad is not responsible for errors in time tables, inconvenience or damage resulting from delayed trains or failure to make connections; schedules herein are subject to change without notice.

Buy Tickets before boarding train and avoid payment of extra charge.

Children. Children under 5 years of age, if accompanied by parent or guardian will be transported without charge. Each child five years of age and under twelve years of age, one-half the adult fare (sufficient to be added if necessary to make child's fare end in next full cent). Each child twelve years of age and over, full adult fare.

Stop-Overs will not be allowed at any station on the New York and Long Branch Railroad or at any point on the Central Railroad of New Jersey between New York and Perth Amboy, inclusive, on tickets reading between New York, Jersey City, Newark or Elizabeth, and New York and Long Branch Railroad stations.

Adjustment of Fares. In case of misunderstanding with Conductors or Agents, pay the fare required, take receipt and communicate with Manager—Passenger Operations, Jersey City 2, N. J.

Redemption of Tickets. Central Railroad of New Jersey one-way and round-trip tickets wholly unused may be redeemed by selling agent within thirty days from date of sale. After thirty days such tickets and all partially used tickets may be presented or mailed to Manager—Passenger Operations, Jersey City 2, N. J. If desired, tickets may be left with any ticket agent who will give receipt and forward to above address for direct settlement with purchaser.

Lost Articles. This Railroad will not be responsible for articles left on trains. Inquiry should be made at nearest Ticket Agency or at the office of the Manager—Passenger Operations, Jersey City 2, N. J.

Time: 12.01 midnight to 12.00 noon is indicated by light-faced type.

12.01 PM to 12.00 midnight is indicated by bold face type.

NEW YORK CITY BUS AND SUBWAY SERVICE

Our New York Terminal, located at Liberty and West Streets (one block south of Cortlandt St.) is convenient to the Eighth Avenue Coach Co. buses leaving from Cortlandt and West Sts., and running via Hudson St., Eighth Ave. and Central Park West to 159th St. and is but a few minutes walk to the Cortlandt St. station of the I.R.T. (Seventh Avenue) and B.M.T. (Broadway) subways and either Fulton or Wall St. station of the I.R.T. (Fourth Ave.-Lexington Ave.) subway and the Fulton-Chambers St. station of the Independent subway system which adjoins Hudson Terminal (Cortlandt St.) by under-cover passageway.

SEASIDE PARK-POINT PLEASANT BUS SERVICE

Bus service between Point Pleasant and Seaside Park and intermediate points is operated by the Coast Cities Coaches Inc. Jersey Central Lines tickets are not honored on these buses.

PASSENGER TRAFFIC REPRESENTATIVES
Jersey City Terminal, Jersey City 2, N. J.

E. L. TOMLINSON, Passenger Traffic Manager
T. F. CLARKIN, Asst. Passenger Traffic Manager
J. J. HITCHELL, General Eastern Passenger Agent

SAVE up to 50%
on round trip fares to
NORTH JERSEY BEACHES
Wednesdays and Weekends (Sat.-Sun.)
June 14 thru Sept. 14, 1958.

A grand opportunity to give the kids the thrill of a trip on a modern Diesel-powered train!

Good on all Jersey Central Lines trains—Wednesdays, going and returning the same day—Weekends, going Saturday or Sunday and returning either Saturday or Sunday the same weekend.

Please ask local Ticket Agent for circular giving complete details.

SEASHORE
TRANS

Passenger Service
Completely Dieselized

EFFECTIVE

APRIL 27, 1958

(CORRECTED JUNE 2)

DAYLIGHT SAVING TIME

In 1958, 11 northbound trains would make a stop at the Union Beach Station on a weekday, six of them before 9:00 a.m.

This oft-used Central Railroad of New Jersey monthly ticket allowed the bearer to commute between Union Beach and New York in July 1928.

Beginning on October 28, 1956, the Jersey Central Railroad operated the latest types of Budd Rail diesel cars on the Atlantic Highlands-Matawan Division. They were used until passenger service was discontinued on October 30, 1966, and the tracks from IFF (International Flavors & Fragrances) to Atlantic Highlands were removed. There had been six daily trains with 55 weekday passengers boarding at Union Beach for all destinations in 1966. The Budd diesel cars are on the right side of the rail equipment at the Atlantic Highlands Station.

64

SPECIAL HOLIDAY SERVICE

—TO—

NEW YORK

and NEWARK

MONDAY, JULY 5, 1943

To accommodate Holiday traffic on above date, extra service will be provided as outlined below:

		P.M.	P.M.	P.M.
East Long Branch	Leave	3.50	6.20	8.15
North Long Branch		3.52	6.22	8.17
Monmouth Beach		3.54	6.24	8.19
Sea Bright		4.01	6.31	8.26
Normandie		f4.03	f6.33	f8.28
Navesink Beach		f4.04	f6.34	f8.29
Highland Beach		f4.06	f6.36	f8.31
Highlands		4.08	6.38	8.33
Water Witch		4.12	6.42	8.37
Hiltons		f4.16	f6.46	f8.41
Atlantic Highlands		4.22	6.50	8.45
Leonardo		4.25	6.53	8.48
Belford		4.29	6.57	8.52
Port Monmouth		4.32	7.00	8.55
Keansburg		4.37	7.05	9.00
Union Beach		4.42	7.10	9.05
Keyport		4.45	7.15	9.09
Matawan		4.50	7.20	9.15
Elizabethport	Arrive	5.17	7.47	9.41
Newark, E. Ferry St.		5.27	7.57	
Newark, Ferry St.		5.30	8.00	9.53
Newark, Broad St.		5.34	8.04	9.57
Jackson Ave. (Jersey City)		5.35	8.08	10.07
Jersey City Terminal		5.44	8.13	10.15
New York, Liberty St.	Arrive	6.02	8.25	10.33
		P.M.	P.M.	P.M.

f—stops on notice to take or leave passengers.

With two rail lines serving Long Branch, it wasn't an accident that the first two hospitals in Monmouth County were located near the train station. Local rail service to Long Branch ended in 1949.

Late Union Beach Mayor and Monmouth County Freeholder Carmen M. Stoppiello assisted in cutting the ribbon to officially open the Henry Hudson Trail on June 3, 1995. The trail, run by the Monmouth County Park System, is on the road bed of the old Central New Jersey Railroad from Matawan to Atlantic Highlands. It was covered with blacktop in November of 1996. Also in the photograph are Eagle Scout Christian Kant of Troop 134 and Adeline Lubkert of the Monmouth County Park System.

Three trolley cars meet at the Campbell Junction station of the Jersey Central Traction Co. in Middletown. (The Dorn Collection.)

"Built in 1903, the new power house, 90-by-90 feet, was erected at Newtown, which is known as the Florence Avenue Station. The boiler room has a capacity of 1,200-horse power." (*Keyport Weekly*, December 15, 1905.) The powerhouse was located next to the railroad to facilitate the delivery of coal needed for the boiler. A trolley company, besides providing local transportation, also brought electricity and electric streetlights to the communities it served. When the Union Beach powerhouse went into operation, the original powerhouse in the old Keyport trolley barn continued to provide electric power for a growing service area. After the trolley company ceased operations on July 28, 1923, the Jersey Central Power & Light Co. acquired control of the local power company on March 28, 1925.

A view from the railroad station shows a closed trolley car crossing the local trestle that was built in September of 1904. "As the trains and trolley cars were in competition with each other for local passengers, the railroad wouldn't permit the trolley cars to cross their tracks at ground level." (*Keyport Weekly*, July 17, 1903.) "The overhead bridge (trestle) just east of Florence Ave Station has a clearance of 23 feet over the Atlantic Highlands Division Railroad tracks, and is 970 feet long. It has an 83-foot through girder span across the tracks." (*Keyport Weekly*, December 15, 1905.) The crossing would have been east of the new Union Beach water tower. The *Keyport Weekly* of September 16, 1904, reported that the trestle and approaches would cost about $20,000. Reports were that it was a very rickety ride across the trestle. (The Dorn Collection.)

This is a back view of the 80-by-300-foot Jersey Central Traction Co. trolley car barn on Florence Avenue, built in the summer of 1907. Five trolley tracks ran into the building. The track on the right side ran into the service area for repairs and painting of three cars. The barn accommodated 30 cars. Later, a trolley shed was constructed to the north of this building. Trolleys from Keyport would come down the north side of Broadway, go around the barn on the south side, and travel east to the trestle and on to Campbell's Junction. The trolley company went out of business on Saturday night, July 28, 1923. The year-round population of the Bayshore area was too small to support the trolley line. During the summer months, they were hard pressed to keep up with the demand. The age of the automobile was starting in the 1920s and local roads were being improved. Route 36 was constructed from Keyport to the Highlands in 1922–23. The back half of this building housed the Union Beach Municipal Water Works from 1927 to March of 1992. Presently it is used by the Union Beach Public Works Department. The front half has housed a number of concerns over the years.

TIME TABLE

In Effect June 25th.

SUBJECT TO CHANGE WITHOUT NOTICE.

✻✻✻✻✻✻✻✻✻✻✻✻✻✻✻✻✻✻

JERSEY CENTRAL TRACTION CO.

OFFICE

KEYPORT, N. J.

✻✻✻✻✻✻✻✻✻✻✻✻✻✻✻✻✻✻

The Jersey Central Traction Company connects with the Central Railroad of New Jersey, the Pennsylvania, Long Branch, Sandy Hook Boat Line, Patten Boat Line and the Merchants' Boat Line to and from New York.

﹗. I. BROWN, Gen. Mgr.	A. R. DIMICK, Supt.

SUMMER SCHEDULE

Keyport, Red Bank and Highlands Division.

First car leaves Keyport 5:00 and Red Bank at 6:00 A. M. Highlands 7:00 A. M. Cars arrive and depart from these points on the hour up to and including 9:00 A. M. After 9:00 A. M. a half hour schedule will be maintained and cars will arrive and depart from Keyport, Red Bank and Highlands on the hour and half hour up to and including 8:30 P. M., after which cars will leave the same points on the hour at 9:00, 10:00, 11:00 and ▮▮▮ P. M., and last cars leave Red Bank and Highlands for Keyport only, at 12 midnight.

Cars, on the hourly schedule, pass through Atlantic Highlands for Highlands fifteen minutes before the hour and from Highlands to Red Bank, Keyport and South and Perth Amboy fifteen minutes after the hour. On the half hour schedule cars meet at Atlantic Highlands fifteen minutes before and fifteen minutes after the hour.

Keyport, South and Perth Amboy Division.

First car from Keyport to South and Perth Amboy at 5:00 A. M. Then on a half hourly schedule leaving Keyport on the hour and half hour up to and including 8:30 P. M., leaving South Amboy five and thirty-five minutes past the hour for Perth Amboy. Then on the hourly schedule from Keyport at 9:00, 10:00 and 11:00 P. M.

First car from Perth Amboy at 6:26 A. M., then on a half hourly schedule up to and including 9:26 P. M., leaving Perth Amboy twenty-six and fifty-six minutes after the hour. Then on the hour schedule from Perth Amboy 9:56, 10:56 and 11:56 P. M. Cars leaving South Amboy for Keyport 6:21 A. M., and every half hour; leaving South Amboy twenty-one and fifty-one minutes past the hour up to and including 9:51. Then on the hour schedule from South Amboy 10:21, 11:21 and 12:21.

Last car from Perth Amboy for Keyport only.

South Amboy---Woodbridge Creek

A. M.

First car from South Amboy at 5:35 A. ▮ Perth Amboy 5:56. Woodbridge Creek 6:11, half hourly leaving South Amboy five and th▮ five minutes past the hour. Perth Amboy tw▮ six and fifty-six minutes past the hour. W▮ bridge Creek eleven and forty-one minutes pa▮ hour up to and including 7:35 from South Am▮

P. M.

First car from South Amboy 3:35. ▮ Amboy 3:56. Then on a half hourly schedu▮ to and including 6:05 P. M. from South Amb▮

First car from Woodbridge Creek 4:11, ▮ half hourly leaving Woodbridge Creek eleven ▮ forty-one minutes past the hour up to and incl▮ 6:41.

Keyport---Matawan Division

First car from Walnut Street to Matawa▮ 5:30 A. M. Next car 5:50; thence 6:30 and ▮ twenty minutes up to and including 11:10 ▮ Last car 12:00.

Matawan---Freneau Division

From Matawan Station first car 5:50 A▮ then every twenty minutes up to and including car 11:10 P. M. Last car from Freneau at ▮ direct to Keyport.

The Jersey Central Traction Com▮ passes through Maurer, Perth Amboy, S▮ Amboy, Morgan, Cliffwood, Keyport, ▮ wan, Freneau, Keansburg, Belford, Mi▮ town, Red Bank, Atlantic Highlands, S▮ Church and Navesink Highlands.

This is a c. 1909 trolley schedule. The Carr Avenue Line in Keansburg was for summer use only and was subsidized by the Keansburg Steamboat Company. The first trip was on July 22, 1914. Later, the line was extended out onto the pier. Campbell's Junction in Middletown was where the trolley cars from the Highlands and Red Bank would meet, with cars going north to Keyport and the Amboys. The trolley lines in the state were connected with each other and you could travel to Trenton, Newark, or other cities in New Jersey.

A Jersey Central Traction Co. trolley car has stopped to pick up a passenger on Highland Avenue in the Highlands. Traffic appears to be very light heading to the beaches the day this photograph was taken.

An open trolley car used in the summer months is shown here at the end of the line on Portland Avenue in the Highlands. Up the hill are the Twin Lighthouses. The Jersey Central Traction Co. colors were green and yellow with white lettering.

The motor men's badges were all odd numbers and the conductors' badges were all even numbers. Also included is a Jersey Central Power & Light Co. badge, numbered 96. All belonged to Joseph H. Collins Sr. of Keyport. The Jersey Central Power & Light Co. purchased the local electric company on March 28, 1925.

A new center door trolley of the Jersey Central Traction Co. is shown here in June 1915 at the Campbell's Junction station. On the back of the postcard it is stated that passengers would pay as they entered the car.

This is the surviving building of the Jersey Central Traction Co.'s new 1903 powerhouse as seen from Florence Avenue. It is one of three buildings owned by GPU in Union Beach.

The Jersey Central Power & Light Company erected this 50-foot-tall arch-shaped Aerial Device Garage in 1971 to service its trucks and hydraulic equipment at the corner of Broadway and Florence Avenue. It was demolished in 1991.

73

These Jersey Central Power and Light Company Line Department workers posed in 1940 on the Poole Avenue side of the powerhouse building. The line department included the following, from left to right: Joseph H. Collins Sr., Fred Seiben, Charles Bowker, Francis Smith, Frank Conway, Frank Briskie, Roy Carney (kneeling), Tony Trebino, Dan Kondrup, J.H. McDonnell, George Spratford, Marvin Torrence, Charles Kinhafer (eyes and hat barely visible), George Hushour, Frank Cook, Milton (Sonny) Fahrer, Lloyd Walling, Ed Walters, E. Irons, unidentified, Ed Wethered, Walter Smith, and Pete Stryker.

Four

COMMUNITY SERVICES

Teacher George W. Aumack stands by the door of the Union Schoolhouse, *c.* 1910. In 1885 the school had 56 scholars.

The Union School District No. 50 one-room schoolhouse built in 1850 served the students in the northern section of Raritan Township into the 1920s. By 1955, the old schoolhouse was converted into a house with an added front porch. The building was later razed for the construction of a new house in 1980. It had stood on the southwest corner of Seventh Street and Florence Avenue.

This interior view of the 1850 Union School District No. 50 one-room schoolhouse with its pot-bellied stove was taken in 1921. During the summer, the school had been renovated and new furniture purchased for Mrs. Marguerite Bogarth's fifth- and sixth-grade class. Along with four classrooms in the Florence Avenue School, the local schools remained overcrowded.

GRADUATION EXERCISES

UNION GRAMMAR SCHOOL
THURSDAY EVENING, JUNE 8, 1922

UNION FIRE HOUSE

Nᵒ 5   **ADMIT ONE**

This ticket for the 1922 graduation exercises held at the Union Firehouse was saved by Mrs. Jessie McKittrick from the graduation of her son, James D. McKittrick. It was almost lost in the fire at her home in 1932.

In 1915, the two-classroom Florence Avenue School was constructed. Two classrooms were added on by October 1917, and two additional rooms were constructed south of the original building and connected with a walkway for January of 1923. Nevertheless, the school remained overcrowded.

This *c.* 1917 photograph was taken on the steps of the Florence Avenue School with Mrs. Compton and her class of fourth, fifth and sixth graders. The principal, Mr. Wells, taught seventh and eighth grades.

The four front classrooms of the Cottage Park School comprised the original school that opened in September 1924. Local residents complained that there were no fire escapes. An addition to the school was built for the 1928 school year.

The three girls standing by the school water pump are, from left to right, Ann Claire Masson, Marilyn Heary, and Isabelle Hedley. Before the borough water system was installed in early 1927, the schools had wells and outhouses. The plaque under the top center windows, "Union School," referred to the Union School District.

Some of the school staff pose during a class trip to Newark Airport around 1940. They are, from left to right, Harold Butterfield (principal,) Kathleen Eckhart, Agnes Jones, Burtina Aumack, and John Cooney (custodian.) Burtina Aumack, daughter of teacher Julia Aumack, graduated Union Beach in 1928, Keyport High School in 1932. As Mrs. Parcels, Burtina would later teach English at Keyport High School until her retirement.

The staff of the school monthly newspaper *Cottage Park Highlights* posed for a photograph in 1941. This was the fourth year the school paper had used this title. Sitting down in front is Thomas Flood. The others are, from left to right, as follows: (first row) Herman Wirth, Marion Chandler, Mary Durka, and Alice Budaway; (second row) Paul Gelhaus (assistant editor), Winnie Johnson, Margaret Brennan, and Edith Masson (assistant editor); (back row) unidentified, Anastasia Koel (editor), Betty Whitaker, Miss Ruby Petty (teacher), Mr. Butterfield (principal), and Henry Klinski. Also on the staff were Pauline Clark, Gloria LaGiglia, Veronica Van Nest, and Ruth Criger. The photograph is from the student-made yearbook of 1941. The Union Beach Memorial Library would like to have copies of the student-made yearbooks for its files.

A 1932 class project on display at the Cottage Park School shows some of the work of the local pupils. The sign says "Mt. Vernon, Washington's Estate. Reproduced by the pupils of the arithmetic classes of grades 5–6 under the direction of Mr. Wells." Reportedly it was made by Mrs. Aumack's class.

Two classrooms were reopened in the Florence Avenue School, north building, for the 1942–43 school year. The building had been closed for nine years because of a decline in enrollment during the Depression and as an economic measure. The Cottage Park School had overcrowded classes of 40 students or more. From 1938 to 1950 the borough hall and police station occupied the two-room south building. By 1950 all the classrooms were once again needed by the school.

The dedication of the Memorial School next to the Cottage Park School on Morningside Avenue took place on November 15, 1957. The original school had ten classrooms as well as an "All-Purpose" room. Six more classrooms were added by September 1958, permitting the school system to return to full sessions. Other additions were made in 1962, 1965, and 1973. This photograph is of the first class to graduate from the school, the class of 1958.

The Cottage Park School was destroyed by fire Saturday morning, February 22, 1964. All of the school records stored in the basement were lost. The fire equipment was at IFF when the fire started, thus valuable time was lost. In 1928, when the addition had been added, the firewall between the two sections wasn't extended to the roof. Classes returned to half sessions.

The new Cottage Park School—four modular classrooms on the site of the old school—was moved into on January 19, 1970.

The original Union Beach Library building was an old cobbler's shop on Union Avenue near Jersey Avenue. The *Keyport Weekly* reported on October 29, 1936, that "the library is to open formally tomorrow." The *Keyport Weekly* of December 10, 1936, reported that "the library is a success. It opened to the public on November 3 and 436 books were borrowed in the first month. It now has 111 members."

The almost-finished library building was dedicated on November 11, 1946. It was dedicated in memory of the 12 borough residents who lost their lives during World War II. A parade had been held in the morning welcoming home 150 veterans of the war. The building was constructed with labor and materials donated by borough residents.

On October 11, 1959, a 20-by-40-foot addition to the Memorial Library, located at 810 Union Avenue, was dedicated. It provided space for a health center and more space for the library. When the library closed in August of 1972 for renovations, the health center moved to the school. In 1989, a 30-by-50-foot addition was dedicated. The new main room is named in honor of the late Leo and Claire Filkin.

The first ambulance was purchased in November 1938 from the Newark City Hospital for $125 by Edward Letwenske and Frederick Clauss. Chartered in November of 1938, the First Aid Squad went into service on May 28, 1939.

The First Aid Squad went into service on May 28, 1939. Members included, from left to right, Joe Kolodziej, George Cowling, Bill Bishop, George Pouzenc, Ed Zahn, Alfred Cowling, Alfred Maier, Clarence McQueen, Gus Dirner, Ted Trembley, Tom Sullivan, George Wirth, and Walter Penrose.

The original home of the Union Beach First Aid Squad on Park Avenue was the old home of the Union Gardens Fire Department. Over the years, the building has been replaced with a new and larger building on the same site.

The Union Beach First Aid Squad Members are shown here in July 1957. They include the following, from left to right: (kneeling) Walter Chomic, Edward Brandigon, Al Cowling, and Harry Chandler; (semi-circle) William Craig, Norman Luettchau, Robert Orr, John McInnes, Charles Dillone, Clarence McQueen Sr., Edward Luettchau Sr., Walter Penrose, George Anderson, Clarence McQueen Jr., Thomas Ward, George Wirth, William Havens, Pat Havens, and Joseph Kolodziej. Absent when the photograph was taken were George Ader, George Sappah, Gus Dirner, John Calandra, and Honorary Members Theodore Trembley, Floyd Leonard, Thomas Perno, Edward Ferrari, and Jack Douglas.

This photograph was featured on the program cover for the first annual dance of the police department, Saturday evening, August 22, 1925, at the Union Avenue Firehouse. The members of the police department shown here include the following, from left to right: (front row) Burtis Aumack (commissioner), Fred Schober (police chief), and James P. McKittrick (commissioner); (back row) Officer William Tighe, Officer Gus Dirner Sr., Sergeant Fred Everson, and Officer Emil Schaefer.

The members of the Union Beach Police Department, including special police, posed for this photo in 1947 on the steps of the borough hall/Florence Avenue School. In the front row, from left to right, are Patrolman Walter Hutton, Sargeant John Sanders, Captain Bill Tighe, and Councilman John J. Muller.

Members of the 1946 Police Cadets pose with Patrolman Walter Hutton and Sergeant John Sanders. They are, from left to right, as follows: (front row) Raymond Bellaran, Bill English, Walter Hutton, John O'Bannon, John Sanders, Louis Bartholomew, and Robert Mount; (back row) Bill Ritt, two unknown cadets, Herbert Davis, Roy Gryner, and Bob Greeley. (The Dorn Collection.)

This interior view shows the police headquarters at 614 Union Avenue around 1952. Police Officer Arthur Gray is on the phone while Sergeant Richard Trembley is at the desk discussing something with Councilman Joe Donnelly. In 1954, a street was named in Haven Park for Donnelly, the mayor, and other councilmen when the last farm in town became a housing development. (The Dorn Collection.)

The Union Beach Police Cadets are standing in front of police headquarters and tax office at Central and Union Avenues in 1959. In the early 1960s, the offices moved to the waterworks building in the old trolley barn. The new borough hall was dedicated in 1981, followed by the police annex in 1984.

The area's first fire company, Union Gardens Fire Co. No. 1, was organized on July 4, 1920. A photograph that was printed backwards shows the members in the late 1930s. Ground was broken for a new firehouse on Park Avenue in May 1931. An addition was added on a few years later. Their original firehouse would later become the home of the First Aid Squad.

Several members of the Union Gardens Fire Co. No. 1 pose for a photograph at a fire department drill sometime in the 1940s. In 1978, a two-bay addition was added to their firehouse. For years now their equipment, a fire truck and a rescue vehicle, has been red and white.

The Union Hose Fire Co. No. 1 with red trucks was organized on April 19, 1921. Their original home was the building at 1234 Florence Avenue. During the 1920s and 1930s, the hall was used for dances, graduations, plays, and parties. A new firehouse was built in 1946 with a two-bay addition added in 1969. This photograph shows members conducting a fund-raising drive in the late 1940s.

This photograph, taken in 1960, shows some of the members of Union Hose Co. No. 1, located at Florence and Poole Avenues. The second oldest fire company in town, it has three trucks in service. The 1951 Mack truck has its own building. Members in the truck are, from left to right, as follows: (front row) Bruce Beaman and Jack Seber; (standing) Robert Baird, John Lambrecht, Chief Frank Schaden, and James MacNamee.

Why do the men of the Union Beach Fire Co. No. 1 have the American flag upside down in this photograph taken in 1928? On November 15, 1922, a meeting was held to organize a fire company east of Flat Creek to be housed in the Lorillard and Union Beach Improvement Association hall at the corner of Union and Cambridge Avenues.

The Union Beach Fire Co. No. 1, with its white fire trucks, marked its 30th anniversary and the dedication of its new firehouse at the corner of Union and Morningside Avenues on Saturday, October 31, 1953. Since this picture was taken in 1957, the upstairs windows have been replaced and new doors installed on the two bays. Their third truck, a 1957 Ward LaFrance, is kept in a bay at the back of their building.

Union Beach Fire Co. No. 1 dedicated a monument to all deceased firemen of the Union Beach Fire Department following the Memorial Day parade on May 31, 1959. The monument is located next to the firehouse.

The Union Beach Fire Co. No. 1 Ladies Auxiliary was organized in February 1925. This photograph may have been taken on the same day as the first fire company picnic but the location of this house is unknown.

Harris Gardens Hose Co. No. 1 was organized on October 15, 1929, to serve the Harris Gardens and Natco sections of Union Beach. This photograph was taken on August 29, 1954, at their 25th anniversary celebration. For a number of years, their fire trucks have been painted powder blue.

In 1971, Department Chief Robert Brunelli and members of the Harris Gardens Fire Co. stand by the 1967 addition to their firehouse. In 1989, a new firehouse was dedicated down the street from their original home on Harris Avenue. The company has a fire truck, a 75-foot aerial ladder truck, and a utility rig.

Mr. Frank Carnelli and his family learn how to drive the Union Beach Fire Co. fire truck in case of a fire in 1947.

Shown here are members of the Union Beach Police Explorer Post 134, organized in 1986. They are, from left to right, as follows: (front row) Mrs. Weinrich, Kelly Smith, Jeanine Jacob, Jackie Shipley, and Mrs. Wooley; (middle row) Pete Weinrich, Mike Kelly, Sean Michaels, Rob Bellino, Brian Dubey, and Robert McIsaac; (back row) Mike Goedecker, Ray McGlyn, Edward McKenna, Shannon Headley, Peter Cazella, and Allan Brunner.

Five

THE BEACHFRONT

Mrs. Stryker poses on the beach in 1925 with her three daughters, sporting the latest style in swimwear.

Local residents enjoy a day at the beach.

In 1932, people used their large cars as dressing rooms along Front Street. In the background are 338 and 334 Front Street. Both buildings now have a second-floor deck on their street side.

"Happy" Sappah is shown here with a camper and his son at Happy Sappah's Camp Ground stand, located on East Point from 1933 to 1944. The charge for camping was 25¢ per day or $1.50 per week for a site (weekends cost 75¢). A water spigot was on site. Rowboats could be rented for 25¢ for an hour or $1 for the day.

Members of Happy Sappah's family pose in front of one of the tents on East Point, which could be rented for a family vacation.

This aerial view, taken in 1935, shows Front Street. The old railroad barge had been pulled in place in May of 1932 to be used by the Union Beach Motor and Yacht Club for their clubhouse. When the club folded and with the end of Prohibition in December 1933, it became Pop Julian's Boat House Tavern, which featured dances, shows, and boxing matches.

In 1932, Ralph Guerra opened a grocery store on Front Street. In this 1942 photograph, Ralph (to the left, with an apron on) is sitting with four customers. His son, Alphonse Jr., who is now retired, is wearing an apron while sitting on the other side of the door. The store is now the home of Pluggy's Place Deli & Catering.

Gala Fall Dance and Floor Show

PRESENTED BY

JOHNNIE MOUNT

Friday Evening, October 19, 1934

To Be Held At

JULIAN'S BOATHOUSE

UNION BEACH, N. J.

Music by STEVE STONEY'S ORCHESTRA

TWO SHOWS—11 P. M. AND 1 A. M.

TICKETS - - - 21 UNION LABEL - - - 25 Cents

This is a ticket for one of many events staged by local resident Johnnie Mount at Julian's Boathouse.

The interior of "Pop" Julian's Boathouse Tavern is shown here. The tavern workers, from left to right, are Ronnie Cassidy, "Pop" William Julian (owner,) and Jerry Julian and Buster Ferguson (bartenders.) Boxing matches, dances, and floorshows presented by Johnnie Mount were held here.

Frank's Stand, *c.* 1932, stood near the intersection of Dock and Front Streets on the beach. Mrs. Josephine Robertello worked here. When owner Frank Carnelli closed the stand, the building was moved and it is now the living room of a house on Sea View Avenue. Frank Jr. is walking over to his sister Alma and 14-year-old cousin, Eleanor Zibetti.

Clayton's Sunoco Service Station at the corner of Florence Avenue and Front Street is all decorated up for a parade. Ceglia Transmissions is now at this location.

This 1930s postcard of Front Street looks toward Dock Street. The only building now on the right side of the street is the Sand Bar Inn. Many of the buildings on the left side have survived over the years.

Front Street is shown here in a 1930s view looking east. The merry-go-round and Pennyland are on the left side.

Charles Goble's store on Front Street was the local branch of the Keyport Post Office from 1938 to 1942. Dorothy Buriell took it over in 1942 at 600 Front Street and then at 310 Union Avenue. Mrs. Elizabeth Rose took it over in 1973 continuing at 310 Union Avenue. Home delivery of mail began on July 2, 1956.

This beach scene postcard taken before the September 1944 hurricane shows a wide beach behind the establishments on Front Street.

The "Great Hurricane" of September 22, 1938, which skirted the Jersey Coast, damaged the Old Boat House Tavern. Another hurricane during the night of September 14, 1944, destroyed the amusement area on Front Street, according to the *Keyport Weekly*.

A view of Front Street looking toward Conaskonk Point shows damage following a hurricane in the early 1950s. In 1954, the original bulkhead was constructed from Florence Avenue along the beach to the homes near Dock Street. Veteran's Memorial Park at the foot of Florence Avenue was dedicated on Memorial Day, May 29, 1955.

The first annual outboard speedboat regatta was held in Union Beach on Sunday, June 12, 1958. The Central Jersey (Outboard) Boating Association, made up of local racing drivers, sponsored the regatta. Frank Fuller, in his 38 J boat, was photographed during his race on the way to winning another trophy. Seventy-nine racing drivers participated in the 1959 regatta.

Some of the boats built by Frank Fuller are shown here along with some of the trophies won by him and his son Chip (Frank Jr.). Frank built the boats upstairs in his garage. The double windows open out so a finished boat can be lowered to the ground.

"Chip" Fuller poses with his boat in the junior division in the 1958 speedboat regatta off Front Street.

This is a Front Street view of "Pop" William Julian's "Old Boathouse." Various hurricanes did damage to the old railroad barge over the years. In 1947, Charles and Stanley Pruchnik purchased the Old Boathouse from John Csik. A fire in April 1950 gutted the old dance hall section. A new boathouse was built on Front Street in August 1953.

Bob Belmonte rebuilt the building in 1986, calling it the Sand Bar Inn. He added an enclosed deck for summer dining with a view of the New York City skyline. Old photographs of Union Beach decorate the walls of the restaurant/tavern.

This view was taken from the Union Avenue Bridge looking north on Matty's Creek in the 1950s. At one time, the creek was lined with small docks and local residents would keep their boats in the water all summer.

Ron Bezek walks along the shoreline by his grandmother's house at low tide in 1952. You can see where the shoreline was in regard to Princess Cottage in comparison to today.

High and dry on the sand bar at the mouth of Matty's Creek in 1962 is the boat *Helen*, with summer resident Frank Carnelli and a family friend along side. Boats can enter and leave Flat Creek only at high tide. The creek is the only place in the borough where a boat can be put in or taken out.

Mr. Frank Carnelli's boat, which had been tied to a dock in Matty's Creek, came to rest in front of a house on Brook Avenue following the 1944 hurricane.

The Union Beach Italian-American Social Club was organized in March 1948 with William W. Marinella as its first president. These members standing outside their clubhouse at 704 Front Street in 1960 are, from left to right, Frank Raccioppi, Anthony Devino, Danny Angelo, Victor Buccino (president), and Leo La Conte. The club was active in the community into the 1970s and sponsored Girl Scout Troop 93.

The Ironside Athletic Club was famous for its clambakes held outside the establishment on Brook Avenue. After the club was destroyed by fire in the 1950s, a new building was constructed on the corner of Prospect and Union Avenues. The club was chartered in the City of Newark before moving down to Union Beach in 1937. Charles Spielmann was the proprietor.

A statue of St. Gabriel stands at the intersection of Union and Front Streets. An Italian mother in Newark vowed that if her son Gabriel returned safely from World War II, she would erect a statue in the Saint's honor. After her son returned, the family moved to Front Street along with St. Gabriel. The property has been sold several times since 1950 but St. Gabriel remains at his post.

This 1940 aerial view shows the beachfront along Front Street with Dock Street in the foreground. Very few empty lots are left in town to build on. Older homes are either improved or removed to provide space for modern housing. Summer homes are a thing of the past. No more neighborhood baseball games on the local empty lot by neighborhood children.

Six
AROUND "THE BEACH"

A photograph taken at the borough's 25th anniversary celebration shows, from left to right, Ella Lambrecht (runner-up) and Janet Rose (Miss Union Beach).

The reviewing stand was built for the 25th anniversary parade in 1950. The mayor at the time was Joseph Scholer. The parade was held on Saturday, July 1, 1950. On Sunday, July 2, various swimming contests were held along with a baby parade and bathing beauty contest. Monday, July 3, was Children's Day, which included running races and a soapbox derby. On Tuesday, July 4, a regatta was held for runabouts, hydroplanes, and Jersey speed skiffs.

Schoolchildren march in the 1934 Memorial Day Parade. Memorial Day parades have a long tradition in town. Union Beach is one of the few towns in the area to keep the tradition alive.

The Union Beach Soccer Club is shown here in 1945. Home games were played at the Cottage Park field. Many of the players lived in the Scotstown area of Union Beach, behind the Florence Avenue School. The ball boy was Bob Pattison. The others, shown here from left to right, are as follows: (front row) Sam Robinson, Ed Ferrari, Robert Sharp, Frank Fleming, Tom Scott, and Jim Stewart; (back row) Harry Joseph, unidentified, Mayor Boyle Pattison (1940–1947 and 1958–1960), Bill Wright, unidentified, unidentified, George Anderson Jr., Bert MacBrayne, and Bill Brown. Jim Boyle was president of the club. Other members included Andy Cameron, James Boyd, David Sands, Joe Napier, and Bill Blair.

This was a WPA (Work Projects Administration) project—to put in curbs and sidewalks along Union Avenue, as well as other streets in town, in December 1936. It provided employment on local projects for men who couldn't find employment during the Great Depression. Residents of Union Beach were hit hard by the Depression. Many lost their homes.

SCRIP **THE BOROUGH OF UNION BEACH**
MONMOUTH COUNTY, NEW JERSEY
ACKNOWLEDGES ITS INDEBTEDNESS TO BEARER
IN THE SUM OF
—— **ONE DOLLAR** —— **$1**
THIS CERTIFICATE IS TRANSFERABLE BY DELIVERY AND BEARS INTEREST
AT THE RATE OF 3% PER ANNUM FROM THE DATE OF ISSUE TO THE
DATE OF ACCEPTANCE IN PAYMENT OF TAXES, ASSESSMENTS OR OTHER
CHARGES WHICH MAY BE DUE TO THE BOROUGH OF UNION BEACH
AND IF NOT SO USED WILL BE PAID AND REDEEMED ON A DATE TO
BE HEREAFTER FIXED BY THE MAYOR AND COUNCIL OF THE BOROUGH
OF UNION BEACH.

BOROUGH OF UNION BEACH   DATE OF ISSUE............................

No. 4073   BY .... _James McFettrick_   COUNTERSIGNED:
BY .... _George A. Joy_
MAYOR   BOROUGH COLLECTOR

This is a copy of $1 scrip, dated April 20, 1936, issued by the borough of Union Beach. As the Depression grew worse, the collection of taxes and water fees dropped off as people lost their jobs and homes. In 1932, less than half of these fees were collected. In order to pay its teachers and employees, the borough was forced to issue scrip. Collection of taxes increased some when the Keyport Banking Co. took over the collection of fees.

THE BOROUGH OF UNION BEACH
MONMOUTH COUNTY, NEW JERSEY
ACKNOWLEDGES ITS INDEBTEDNESS TO BEARER
IN THE SUM OF
———— **FIVE DOLLARS** ———— **$5**
THIS CERTIFICATE IS TRANSFERABLE BY DELIVERY TO THE
DATE OF ACCEPTANCE IN PAYMENT OF TAXES, ASSESSMENTS
OR OTHER CHARGES WHICH MAY BE DUE TO THE BOROUGH
OF UNION BEACH AND IF NOT SO USED WILL BE PAID AND
REDEEMED ON A DATE TO BE HEREAFTER FIXED BY THE
MAYOR AND COUNCIL OF THE BOROUGH OF UNION BEACH.

BOROUGH OF UNION BEACH   Date of Issue:

BY   COUNTERSIGNED:
BY

James McFettrick   _George A. Joy_
Mayor   Borough Collector

The second series of Union Beach scrip was dated April 18, 1933. The second series was redeemable at full face value at the bank on June 23, 1933.

Marching in the 1940 Memorial Day Parade are the members of the Pride of Monmouth Lodge No. 12 of the Daughters of America. The chapter was chartered on March 7, 1927, and was active in the community up to when it merged with another lodge in 1975. In the background, Mr. Littleton Bishop is standing out in front of the A&P store at Union and Central Avenues. The Crystal Bar is across the street at 711 Union Avenue.

A parade in 1950 passes the home and barbershop of Matty Begdanobie, located next to the bridge on Union Avenue. On government maps, this bridge crosses Flat Creek; on old survey maps of the area, it is Conaskunk Creek; but to local residents, it is Matty's Creek. People now fish from the site of the old barbershop. Many people will remember that Matty also raised and sold canaries.

A baby parade joins the Memorial Day parade at the Florence Avenue School in the late 1950s.

COLONIAL
DOOR STOPER

A local girl poses for a picture in front of the barn by John Mount's store elaborately dressed as a "Colonial Door Stoper."

The dedication of the "Lest We Forget" monument for Union Beach residents in World War I took place at the Florence Avenue School on July 4, 1940.

The American Legion Post 321 was chartered on July 24, 1945. Many of the members of the Associated Veterans of American Wars Post No. 1, Union Beach, chartered on December 6, 1925, joined the new American Legion post. The American Legion moved to the former Tetro's Casino on Front Street. The new hall was dedicated on October 2, 1959.

The American Legion Post 321 Firing Squad on Memorial Day in 1956 took part at the wreath laying ceremony at the Lest We Forget monument at Florence Avenue School. In 1958, the monument was moved to Veterans Memorial Park at the foot of Florence Avenue, which had been dedicated on Memorial Day, 1955.

Joseph Gallopo, his wife, Lydia, and their children Mandy and Angie sit in front of Gallopo's Esso Gas Station on Florence Avenue at Ninth Street. Across the street was Clayton's Meat Market. In the 1970s, it became McGrogan & Sons Exxon. The photograph was taken around 1948.

Snow is shown here being cleared from Gallopo's Gas Station in 1961. The pumps were located next to Florence Avenue. On the right, is Clayton's Meat Market at Ninth Street.

Mr. and Mrs. James P. McKittrick are shown here in 1944. Mr. McKittrick was a councilman in 1925, was elected mayor in November of 1925, and was reelected in 1929, serving until 1938. He was a charter member of the Democratic Club, the Associated Veterans of American Wars Post No. 1, financial secretary of the Union Beach Fire Co. and served on the committee in favor of having the new borough named Union Beach instead of Lorillard. In 1924, Mr. and Mrs. McKittrick worked to establish the Congregational Church. As mayor, trying to keep the new borough afloat during the Depression, with bonds for the new water plant to pay and with so many people unable to pay their taxes, was a very difficult situation.

The dedication of the Joseph A. Scholer Memorial Park took place on September 26, 1965, at the intersection of Spruce, Prospect, and Fifth Streets. The 3-acre park was the result of sanitary landfill and is named for the late Mayor Joseph Scholer. It contains a baseball field, swings, tennis, volleyball courts, and play equipment for children. In 1983, the park received the First Place Charles M. Pike Annual Achievement Award for park and recreation facilities.

One of the projects of the Union Beach Lions Club was the establishment of baseball teams for the youth of the community. They sponsored the Lions baseball team as part of this project. In 1958, the local teams joined the National Little League. This photograph is of a parade at the start of baseball season with a Little League queen riding in the convertible.

The members of BSA Troop 56, at the Forestburg Scout Reservation, were photographed in 1959 with their leaders, Harry Briel and Frank Mirro. The first local Scout troops were organized in April 1923 in the Union section of town. Mr. John Radin was the scoutmaster of Troop 7, while Mrs. Radin was the leader of Girl Scout Troop No. l. Boy Scout Troop 56 was chartered March 12, 1925.

An Eagle Court of Honor was held by Troop Post 56 in 1955 for new Eagle Scouts Cornelius Hourahan, Robert Ainslie, and William Wagner. On the left of the photograph are Post Leader Frank Mirro Jr. and new Life Scouts Charles Kolodziej and Donald Kline. Some of the Eagle Scouts over the years include Joseph Calandriello in 1930; Richard Krapp in 1947; Donald Kline in 1956; George Matthews Jr., Edward Griswold, John Cooney, Ronald Gilmartin, and Frederick Tavenor in 1961; Frank Briel in 1962; and Ronald Bezek in 1964.

The members of the Union Beach Sea Scouts Sea Wolf Ship 56 are pictured on a 1949 campout at Spermaceti Cove, Sandy Hook. The scouts embarked from Keyport aboard Skipper Frank Flynn's 30-foot yawl sailboat and on Bill Bishop's outboard motor boat. Pictured here are, from left to right, Ron Reyes, Bill Ainslie, Bob Davis, Bob Pattison, Clifford Gildawie, Bob Hyer, George Ainslie, Joe Calandra, George Brown, Ray Klein, Herb Klein, and Skipper Frank Flynn.

The McKittrick Foundry was first started in the garage of Thomas McKittrick on Park Avenue. In 1946, a foundry was constructed on Spruce Street near the school for the manufacture of ornamental cast-iron lampposts, their popular jockey hitching posts, etc. The business closed in the late 1950s. The building has since been enlarged and is now used by another firm.

Shown here are the ground-breaking ceremonies for the Bayshore Regional Sewerage Authority wastewater treatment plant at Oak and Eighth Streets, Union Beach. Built on 11 acres, the plant went into operation in 1974 serving four towns, with a capacity of 6 million gallons per day. Expansion of the plant was completed in early 1996 to manage 16 million gallons a day from all or parts of eight communities. Pictured, from left to right, are Paul Smith, Dave Cohen, Fred Varlese, Andy Simonsen, Joseph Morales, Wallace Taylor, and Al Hennessy (mayor of Union Beach).

The Union Beach Fire Department Junior Drum and Bugle Corps was organized in 1950. Their first parade was on a rainy day in Spring Lake. Their original uniform was white shirts, jeans, and black shoes. In 1951, the first uniforms were purchased and a photograph taken at Cottage Park School. Financed by the four fire companies, they maintained a busy schedule. On Memorial Days during the 1950s, the Union Beach parade was their third parade of the day. The local parade would line up and wait for the buses to arrive from Keansburg with the two local bands. The band practiced on Tuesday and Thursday nights.

The Union Beach Fire Department Junior Drum and Bugle Corps is shown here marching down Union Avenue in 1958. Parades would begin at Broadway and Florence Avenue and, after passing the Union Beach Memorial Library, would end at the American Legion hall on Jersey Avenue.

The Community Drum and Bugle Corps, organized in 1954, was the second band in town during the 1950s. Mike Reardon was a drum instructor and Walter Beesley the bugle instructor and business manager.

In June 1966, the Union Beach Firesiders Junior Drum and Bugle Corps became the Bayshore Buccaneers Junior Drum and Bugle Corps, sponsored by the Harris Gardens Fire Co. Membership was opened to youth of the Bayshore area and practice was held in the Memorial School gym. Dances were held to raise funds for the band.

In 1957, the Union Beach Lions baseball team defeated the Cliffwood Angels for the Monmouth County championship. Their sponsor was the Union Beach Lion's Club with Phil Cassidy as team manager. They are, from left to right, as follows (front row) Michael Petito, Jim Beutel, Ron Gilmartin, Bill Kohlbecker, and Robert Samsel; (middle row) Bill Wilson, Andy Cocossa, Steve Ruby, Don Gilmartin, and Jan Nappie; (back row) Albert Kingetter, Dan Hourahan, Tom Walsh, and Bill Trembley. In 1958, the local teams joined the National Little League.

An ad appeared in the July 25, 1947 edition of *the Union Beach Record* for Veterans Hi-Way Furniture Store of Caroline and Earl Von Stade. Later, it became Carrie's Juvenile Highway Furniture Store. A number of years ago, the roof was lowered on the second-floor attic, eliminating the front top windows. The building now houses a video store and sub shop.

Back in the 1920s, Melville D. Stokes ran the Midway Service Station at Stone Road and Seagate Avenue. Later it became Angus Orr & Son Paint Supplies and Hardware and an Amoco gas station. In the fifties, it was Orr's Paint and Wallpaper Store. The house has since been turned around, moved back, and lifted up, with a new store on the ground level. Members of the Orr family now run three businesses at what is known as "Orr's Corner."

This aerial photograph of Union Beach in 1940 shows the 1927 water tower. The 150-foot-tall landmark appeared on local nautical maps. During World War II, the name of the town was painted over to reduce its chance of being used as a landmark by the enemy. The tower was dismantled in the summer of 1988. A new, 100-foot-tall, 1.5-million-gallon water tower that is located near Memorial School went into service in September 1980. The old water tower has been replaced by a modern home at 549 Clark Avenue.

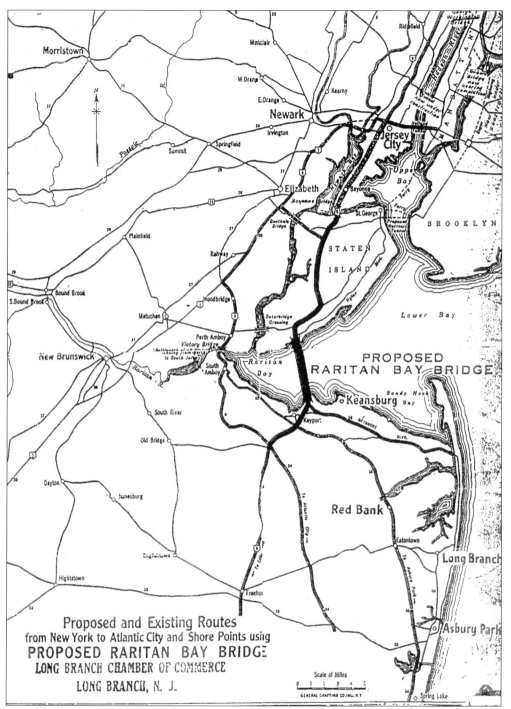

Proposed and Existing Routes
from New York to Atlantic City and Shore Points using
PROPOSED RARITAN BAY BRIDGE
LONG BRANCH CHAMBER OF COMMERCE
LONG BRANCH, N. J.

What if it had been built? A very serious proposal to construct a bridge from Princess Point, Staten Island, to East Point was championed by State Senator E. Donald Sterner of Belmar from 1929 into the 1960s. The Keyport and Long Branch Chambers of Commerce as well as the New York Assembly and New Jersey Legislature endorsed it in 1935. The Port Authority rejected it in 1932 for not being financially feasible and did so again in 1962.